DATE DUE

This Book Belongs to:

Bone Poems

Also by Jeff Moss

The Butterfly Jar
The Other Side of the Door
Bob and Jack: A Boy and His Yak
Hieronymus White
The Dad of the Dad of the Dad of Your Dad

Bone
Poems

by Jeff Moss
Illustrated by Tom Leigh

American Museum of Natural History

WORKMAN PUBLISHING • NEW YORK

Library of Congress Cataloging-in-Publication Data

Moss, Jeffrey
    Bone poems / by Jeff Moss; illustrated by Tom Leigh.
    p.   cm.
    ISBN 0-7611-0884-X
    1. Dinosaurs—Juvenile poetry. 2. Extinct animals—Juvenile poetry. 3. Children's poetry, American.
4. Humorous poetry, American. [Dinosaurs—Poetry.
2. Prehistoric animals—Poetry. 3. American poetry.] I. Leigh, Tom, ill. II. Title.
PS3563.088458B66   1997
811' .54–DC21
                                                            97-15743
                                                            CIP
                                                            AC

Published by
Workman Publishing Company, Inc.
708 Broadway
New York, New York 10003-9555

Manufactured in the United States of America
First printing July 1997
10 9 8 7 6 5 4 3

For Alexis, Linda and Bill
—J.M.

For Susanna
—T.L.

I am grateful to the paleontologists at the American Museum of Natural History for their careful help in my attempt to make these poems scientifically accurate, as well as for their sense of humor and kind understanding of the occasional small liberty taken due to a desperate need for a rhyme. Also, it should be noted that as scientists find more fossils and learn more about them, ideas and theories may change. Just think of the poor *Brontosaurus,* who has the distinction of having become extinct twice. —J.M.

Bone
Poems

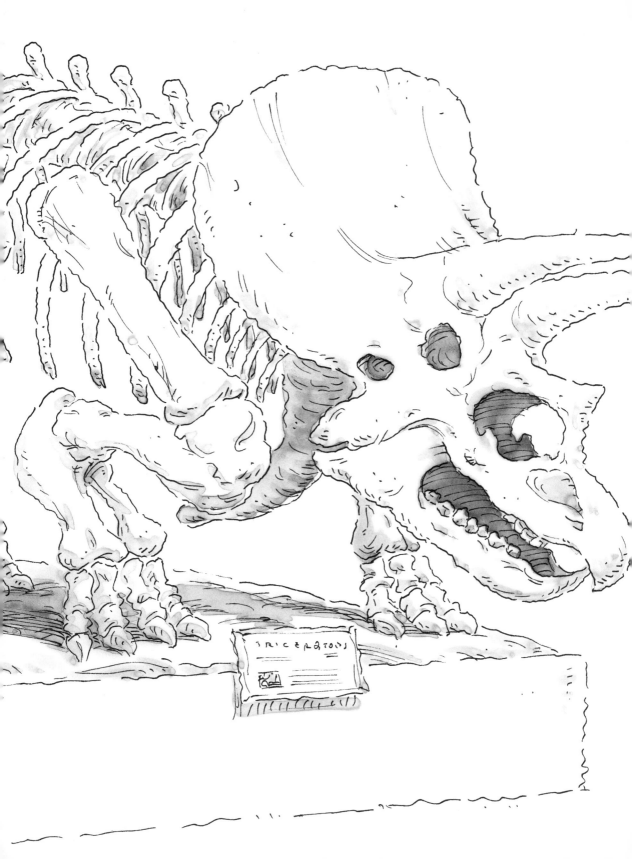

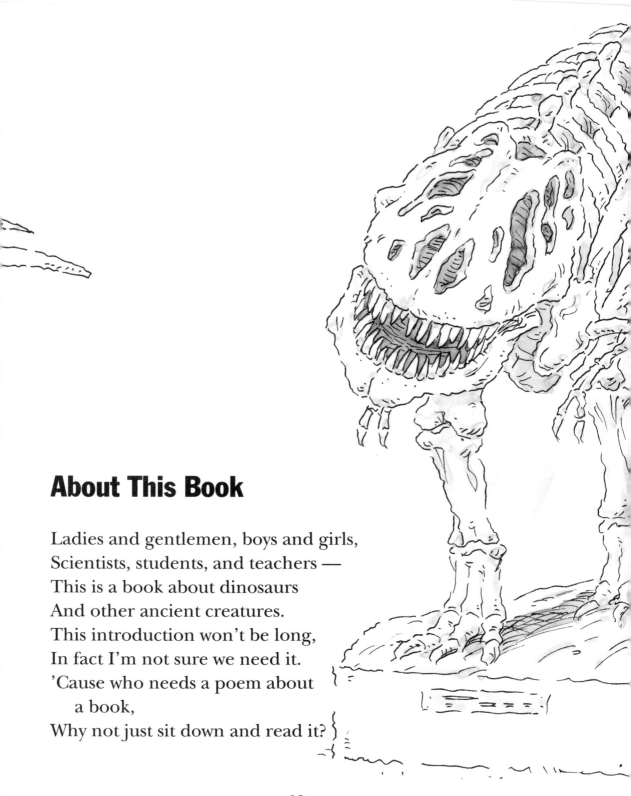

About This Book

Ladies and gentlemen, boys and girls,
Scientists, students, and teachers —
This is a book about dinosaurs
And other ancient creatures.
This introduction won't be long,
In fact I'm not sure we need it.
'Cause who needs a poem about
    a book,
Why not just sit down and read it?

Eating Problem #1
(Apatosaurus)

Apatosaurus was really quite large,
As high as a building, as wide as a barge.
But his mouth was quite tiny, this huge quadruped,
So each day he woke in his dinosaur bed
With a very big problem inside his small head:
How could he keep his great body well fed?
How could he avoid the unpleasant condition
Of dinosaur hunger or worse, malnutrition?
The answer is simple, I'm happy to say.
For hours and hours and hours each day,
He did what you'd do in a similar state
With a mouth very small and a body so great —
He just ate, ate, ate, ate, ate, ate, ate, ate and…

… ate.

Ankylosaurus

All covered with armor the *Ankylosaurus*
Moved with a clunk and a *Clankylosaurus.*
He stood in a stream as he *Drankylosaurus*
And looked like an old army *Tankylosaurus.*

Of course, to be perfectly *Frankylosaurus,*
He had quite a low dino *Rankylosaurus.*
His small mind was often a *Blankylosaurus.*
His smell? Sad to say it, he *Stankylosaurus.*

When down by the old river *Bankylosaurus,*
His young brother's tail he would *Yankylosaurus,*
And this naughty dinosaur *Prankylosaurus*
Might well cause his parents to *Spankylosaurus.*

Time passed and his high spirits *Sankylosaurus*
As dinosaur numbers all *Shrankylosaurus.*
So now I'll say bye-bye and *Thankylosaurus*
'Cause that's all I know about *Ankylosaurus.*

America, the Beautiful Home of Dinosaurs

In the time we call Cretaceous,
Skies were beautiful and spacious
But there were no deer or antelope at play.
Yet *Triceratops* were roaming
Through the hills of old Wyoming—
There were dinosaurs throughout the U.S.A.

Great *Tyrannosaurus rexes*
Lived deep in the heart of Texas,
Though the folks from Texas sure are glad they've gone.
Stegosaurs roamed Colorado
("Eat those plants!" was once their motto).
And in South Dakota lived *Iguanodon*.

You can bet a big banana
Allosaurs in old Montana
Left their massive footprints in the ancient stones.
Scuttelosaurus, itty-bitty,
Made her home near Salt Lake City
Out in Utah where they found her little bones.

Dinos lived in North Dakota,
Massachusetts, Minnesota—
Old New Jersey was the home of hadrosaur.
And it's really quite amazing
When you think of dinos grazing
On your lawn two hundred million years before.

So let's cheer them in a chorus—
Every dinosaur or saurus—
They're American as home-baked apple pies.
And our last historic fact'll
Be a large pterodactyl
Making circles in our beautiful spacious skies.

Bones

Bones are important,
They do a big job.
Without them, you'd be just
A big squooshy blob.

The Arms of Deinocheirus

They found the bones of two huge arms,
Two arms and nothing more—
The arms of *Deinocheirus*,
An amazing dinosaur.
They took their pencils, did some math,
And said, "My, aren't we clever?
With arms so large, this chap might be
The biggest dino ever!"
But since the arms were all they found,
Their thoughts might be amiss.
My guess is *Deinocheirus*
Might have looked a lot…

... like this.

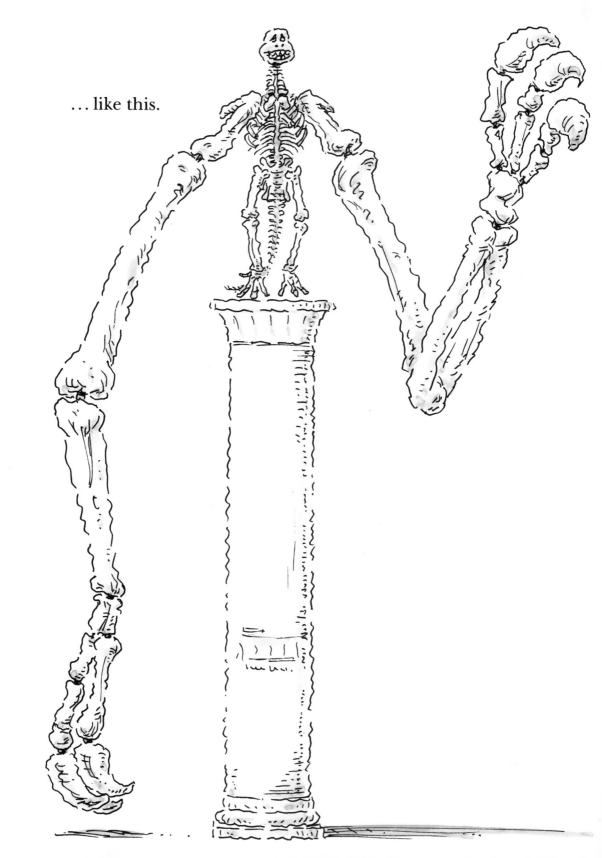

True Colors
(Something to Think About
If It's True That Birds Are
Descended from Dinosaurs)

What colors were the dinosaurs?
Well, no one's ever seen one.
Some think that if they saw a dino
It might be a green one.
But here's another theory—
Think of birds and then you'll know
That these are the true colors
Of the dinos long ago.

There were:
Purple spotted stegosaurs,
And blue *Iguanodons,*
There were orange *Oviraptors,*
Bright red *Hypsilophodons,*
And each pink *Tyrannosaurus*
Had a yellow polka dot —
And there you have the colors
Of the dinosaurs... (Or not.)

Anatotitan

Anatotitan had oodles of teeth,
Hundreds on top and more hundreds beneath.
If someone passed by and said, "What are you doing?"
The most likely answer would be "Ssh! I'm chewing!"
Now, back in those days, with no dentists to mention,
Nature came up with a clever invention.
If ever he broke, cracked, or injured his teeth,
Wonder of wonders, new teeth were beneath!
Just teeth, teeth, and more teeth, how strange and exciting,
A dinosaur set for a lifetime of biting.
Anatotitan—he must have been scary
(Especially if you were the dino Tooth Fairy).

A (Mostly) Dinosaur Alphabet

A is for *Ankylosaurus,*
Brachiosaur starts with B.
Carnosaur's quite a fine C word,
Diplodocus starts with a D.
E is for *Edmontosaurus,*
F is for fossil, you know.
Genasaur is a big G word
Who plodded the earth long ago.
H is for *Herrerasaurus,*
Iguanodon starts with an I.
Jurassic still starts with a J sound
Though millions of years have gone by.
K is for old *Kentrosaurus,*
Lambeosaur starts with L.
Megalosaur is an M word,
And a meat-eating dino as well.
Nodosaur starts with an N sound,
For O, *Oviraptor* rings true.
Protoceratops tops all the P words,
Of course, *Quetzalcoatlus* is Q.
Rhoetosaur starts with an R sound,
Stegosaur starts with an S.
T is for *Tyrannosaurus*
Who "rex" things and makes them a mess.

U is a huge *Ugrosaurus,*
Velociraptor starts with a V.
W is for *Wannanosaurus,*
But it's harder with X, Y, and Z.
Xiphactinus may be an X word,
But it's not quite as fine as we'd wish
'Cause *Xiphactinus* isn't a dino,
It's a gigantic fanged killer fish.
For Y, we're in luck with *Youngina,*
For Z, what's a person to do?
Except to say *Zalamdalestes**
(That's better than zebra or zoo).
This alphabet's finally over,
Recite it yourself for a change.
It's a pretty great thing to
    show off with
Or to prove you're a little
    bit strange.

*Actually, *Zalamdalestes* is a little furry mammal, about the
size of a mouse, who lived at the same time as the dinosaurs.
But it's such a great Z word, who could leave it out?

The Jellyfish and The Clam

Said the clam to the pink jellyfish,
"You're no more than a lump of wet squish!
You've no backbone or brain,
You're too dull to explain,
When they look at you, people go 'Ish!'"

Said the jellyfish back to the clam,
"I may look like thin raspberry jam,
But you're just a thick shell
And you don't even jell,
So I'm happy to be what I am!"

Well, I say let's give three big cheers
For these two and their lengthy careers.
Though they both may be dull,
With no spine and no skull,
Still they've lasted a half-billion years!

The Horn

Parasaurolophus had a huge hollow horn
Rising from the top of her head.
She blew air through it like a big trombone,
For miles the sound would spread.
Her kids would always get annoyed
At six o'clock each day —
'Cause who needs a mom yelling "DINNER TIME!!"
From thirteen miles away?

Quetzalcoatlus

Lots of strange creatures have flown through the skies,
Hummingbirds, pelicans, big dragonflies.
But truly the strangest that I ever knew
Was a huge flying reptile who starts with a Q.

Quetzalcoatlus,
Oooh, what a thing!
Quetzalcoatlus,
With a twenty-foot wing!
He soared through the air,
He was ready to pounce —
Quetzalcoatlus,
So hard to pronounce!

He weighed more than you, he was quite a big guy,
Like a glider he swooped through the dinosaur sky,
High in the clouds over ancient New York,
What is that? A lizard? An airplane?? A stork???

No, it's
Quetzalcoatlus,
Oooh, what a thing!
Quetzalcoatlus,
With a twenty-foot wing!

He soared through the air,
He was ready to pounce —
Quetzalcoatlus,
So hard to pronounce!

If you want to see him, a good place to look
  Is inside your library's dinosaur book.
    Or else on a show called "Amazing But True!"
      You'll find the huge reptile who starts
        with a Q.

Quetzalcoatlus,
Oooh, what a thing!
Quetzalcoatlus,
With a twenty-foot wing!
He soared through the air,
He was ready to pounce —
Quetzalcoatlus,
So hard to pronounce!

Bye-Bye, Brontosaurus

Ever since scientists began studying dinosaurs,
One of their favorites
Was the *Brontosaurus.*
Now there is no *Brontosaurus* anymore.
Here's what happened.

For years,
Scientists kept finding
Brontosaurus bones.
They kept talking about
Brontosaurus this
And *Brontosaurus* that
And *Brontosaurus* blah-blah
Till one day they discovered
That the bones of the *Brontosaurus*
Were the same as some bones
From a different dinosaur they had discovered earlier.
They had called this other dinosaur *Apatosaurus.*
Well, it turned out that *Brontosaurus* and *Apatosaurus*
Were one and the same dinosaur.

So, even though for years and years
Everybody had been talking about
Brontosaurus this
And *Brontosaurus* that
And *Brontosaurus* blah-blah,
The scientists said:
"From now on, all the dinos we used to call *Brontosaurus*
Are going to be called *Apatosaurus.*"

Stop and think about that.

It's kind of like
All your life your name was Jane,
And everyone said, "Hi, Jane," and "Goodbye, Jane,"
And "Clean up your room, Jane,"
And "What's your favorite song, Jane?"
And then one day they said,
"You know what, Jane?
From now on your name is Bill."

It's a good thing *Brontosaurus* are extinct,
Otherwise they would probably be very confused.

BRONTOSAURUS
APATOSAURUS

Eating Problem #2
(Brachiosaurus)

Brachiosaurus stood forty feet tall,
But the teeth that he had couldn't chew well at all.
He'd chomp off some leaves, but he'd swallow them whole,
Which isn't much good when digestion's your goal.
Yet *Brachiosaurus* was sly as a fox.
To help with his problem, the big guy ate rocks.
That's right, I said rocks. No, he wasn't a dummy,
Those rocks helped him grind up the leaves in his tummy.
So next time a science test asks you the question
"Name someone who eats rocks to help with digestion,"
Say *"Brachiosaurus!"* and you'll be a winner
(The guy who eats rock-burgers each night for dinner).

Gotta Find a Footprint

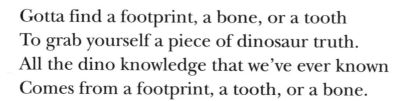

Gotta find a footprint, a bone, or a tooth
To grab yourself a piece of dinosaur truth.
All the dino knowledge that we've ever known
Comes from a footprint, a tooth, or a bone.

A tooth can tell you what a dino would eat,
A sharp tooth tells you that he dined on meat.
A blunt tooth tells you that she dined on plants.
No teeth at all? Well, perhaps they slurped ants.

Gotta find a footprint, a bone, or a tooth
To grab yourself a piece of dinosaur truth.
All the dino knowledge that we've ever known
Comes from a footprint, a tooth, or a bone.

Footprints can tell you a dinosaur's size,
And how fast he ran when he raced with the guys.
Count all the footprints, you'll easily see
If he traveled alone or with a family.

Gotta find a footprint, a bone, or a tooth
To grab yourself a piece of dinosaur truth.
All the dino knowledge that we've ever known
Comes from a footprint, a tooth, or a bone.

Her bones will tell you if she stood up tall,
If she had a big tail or no tail at all.
Put the bones together and see how they'll look—
Pretty enough to get their picture took!

Yeah, gotta find a footprint, a bone, or a tooth
To grab yourself a piece of dinosaur truth.
All the dino knowledge that we've ever known
Comes from a footprint, a tooth, or a bone.

Pachycephalosaurus

A thick-headed reptile with a skull hard as stone,
A very small brain 'neath a huge piece of bone.
When he got angry at something you said,
Pachy would butt you with his big bony head.
Now, sorry to say, but when you're a head-butter
Eventually one thing will lead to anutter,
And as a result of persistent head-butting
A dinosaur's brain may become good-for-nutting.
So though Pachy's head was the strongest head yet,
If you asked, "What's your name?" He'd say,
"Duh…I forget."

Dinosaur Math Quiz

Monoclonius, *Triceratops*, and *Pentaceratops* are all dinosaurs with horns on their heads. Each one has a different number of horns:

Monoclonius + *Triceratops* = 4 horns
Monoclonius + *Pentaceratops* = 6 horns
Triceratops + *Pentaceratops* = 8 horns

1) How many horns does each dinosaur have?
2) How many horns does each dinosaur have if they are on three trains traveling toward each other at the speed of 100 miles per hour?
3) What is stuff like this doing in a poetry book anyway?

Something Else to Think About If It's True That Birds Are Descended from Dinosaurs

Tyrannosaurus walked down the street
He opened his mouth and roared...

Tweet! Tweet!

Words That Describe the Eating Habits of Two Dinosaurs and My Cousin

Carnivorous means that you eat only meat
Like the gigantic fearsome *T. rex.*
Herbivorous means that you eat only plants
Like the brachiosaurs with long necks.
But I've got a word to describe Cousin Pete
Whose strange eating habits arise —
Frenchfrivorous tells you about what he'll eat,
Since all that he eats is french fries.

I'm Going to Ask a Stegosaur to Dinner

I'm going to ask a stegosaur to dinner
Although her manners aren't too polite,
Although I know she'll slobber on her napkin
And crush the chair she sits on every night.
Although she won't make clever conversation,
Although she'll drop a glass or break a plate,
The reason for my eager invitation
Is she happens to love something that I hate.
It isn't that she loves Ms. Orloff's math class,
And same as me, she doesn't like to dance.
But here's where stegosaur and I are different:
She loves to eat green vegetables and plants.
I know she'll hate the burgers Mom is cooking.
She'll never eat Dad's gooey
    toasted cheese,
But each night when
    my parents aren't
    looking…
She'll scarf up
    all my broccoli
    and peas.

STEGGY

An Ancient Horse

Hyracotherium, a tiny horse,
Lived millions of years ago.
He measured just twelve inches high,
So what I'd like to know—
Did paleontologists ever find,
Near where that horse was at,
Some eensy-weensy boots and spurs
And a teeny cowboy hat?

Crocodiles, Turtles, Beetles, and Frogs

Crocodiles, turtles, beetles, and frogs
Were here before hadrosaurs, monkeys, or dogs.
Yes, millions of years before chickens or hogs
There were crocodiles, turtles, beetles, and frogs.

When the earth still was young, they were just the same way.
Frogs all said "Ribit!" like frogs do today.
Shells still were "outer" and turtles were "inner,"
And crocodiles smiled as they eyed you for dinner.

Oh, crocodiles, turtles, beetles, and frogs,
For millions of years they've been crawling on logs.
They've swum through the swamplands and
    bogged through the bogs,
Those crocodiles, turtles, beetles, and frogs.

A beetle's your elder, so please do not hurt
That brown one who just crawled inside of your shirt.
And frogs are a million years older than us,
So please give that froggie your seat on the bus.

Oh, crocodiles, turtles, beetles, and frogs
Survived floods and glaciers and snowstorms and fogs.
Hooray for old bullfrogs and young polliwogs!
Yay! Crocodiles, turtles, beetles, and frogs.

Dimetrodon's Sail

Dimetrodon had a big sail on his back,
Its purpose may leave you confused,
For several wise scientists do not agree
On just how that big sail was used.

Some think that the sail kept *Dimetrodon* warm
As he turned it full face toward the sun.
The heat from the sail made him comfy
    as toast
Till after his sunbath was done.

Others believe that *Dimetrodon*'s sail
Was used to attract a new mate,
A little like showing off new clothes
    you've bought,
As if to say, "Don't I look great!"

Those are the things that the scientists think,
But I think at least one thing more.
And the thing that I think, I think is the thing
That the great big sail really was for.

Dimetrodon, I think, would jump
in the sea,
He would raise his great sail, then
he'd float,
Then his kids would jump on and
they'd go for a ride
On the first prehistoric sailboat!

Ostracoderms

Ostracoderms were ancient fish
Who had no jaws to chew.
With open mouths their food was slurped
As water filtered through.
Perhaps that's why ostracoderms
Kept such a pleasant mood —
They never had to hear their moms
Say, "Henry, chew your food!"

Incorrect

A dinosaur cheerfully winked,
And said, "I will not be extinct!
I'm too wise, I'm too clever,
I'll be here forever!"
(He wasn't as smart as he thinked.)

Cold Enough

Nobody knows for sure what happened to the dinosaurs,
But some people think that about seventy million years ago
The weather got a bit colder all over the earth.
Not *that* cold,
But *cold enough*
So that lots and lots of trees died.
Not freezing cold,
But *cold enough*
So that the plant-eating dinosaurs died
Because there weren't enough trees left for them to eat.
Not an ice age or anything,
But still *cold enough*
So that the meat-eating dinosaurs died
Because there were no plant-eating dinosaurs left for them
    to feed on.

So…
It is possible that
After one hundred fifty million years of ruling the earth,
Dinosaurs vanished and became extinct
Because the weather got *just enough* colder.

So next time your mom tells you
To wear your warm hat and gloves,
Pay attention.

Hippos and Elephants: Two Stories That Are Probably True (Except Maybe the Parts About Talking and Thinking)

Once upon a time, millions of years ago, there was a creature about the size of a big rhinoceros. His neck was very short. His legs were extremely strong, but they didn't bend very well. One day he was thirsty, so he hurried to the edge of the river, but because his legs wouldn't bend and his neck was so short, his mouth couldn't reach down to the water and he couldn't get a drink,

However ...

STORY #1

THE CREATURE THOUGHT AND THOUGHT FOR A WHILE UNTIL HE SAID, "HMMMM, I HAVE AN IDEA.

I'LL WADE INTO THE WATE[R] ALL THE WAY UP TO MY SHOULDERS. THAT WAY I'L[L] BE ABLE TO GET MY DRINK AND IT WON'T MATTER TH[AT] MY NECK IS SHORT AND M[Y] LEGS DON'T BEND."
SO THAT'S WHAT HE DID.

STORY #2

THE CREATURE THOUGHT AND THOUGHT FOR A WHILE UNTIL HE SAID, "HMMMM, I HAVE AN IDEA.

IF I STRETCH AND STRETC[H] AND STRETCH MY NOSE, MAY[BE] THEN I'LL BE ABLE TO GET [A] DRINK AND IT WON'T MATTE[R] THAT MY NECK IS SHORT A[ND] MY LEGS DON'T BEND."
SO THAT'S WHAT HE DID.

HEN, AS YEARS AND YEARS AND YEARS WENT BY, HE THOUGHT AND THOUGHT SOME MORE UNTIL HE SAID, "HMMMM, I HAVE ANOTHER IDEA. FROM NOW ON, I'LL JUST STAY IN THE WATER MOST OF THE TIME. THEN I CAN HAVE A DRINK WHENEVER I WANT ONE, AND I CAN HAVE A NICE TIME SWIMMING, TOO." SO THAT'S WHAT HE DID.

AND EVENTUALLY HE BECAME VERY MUCH LIKE THE HIPPOS WE KNOW TODAY.

THE END

THEN, AS YEARS AND YEARS AND YEARS WENT BY, HIS NOSE GOT A LITTLE BIT LONGER AND LONGER AND LONGER UNTIL AFTER A FEW MILLION YEARS, HE HAD A VERY LONG TRUNK THAT HE COULD STICK INTO THE WATER TO GET A DRINK WHENEVER HE WANTED.

AND EVENTUALLY HE BECAME VERY MUCH LIKE THE ELEPHANTS WE KNOW TODAY.

THE END

A Change of Mind

A giant ancient fish made up
His mind to live on land.
He spoke of his desires
To a friend who'd understand:
"I've had it with the ocean,
I must travel and explore!"
With that he flipped a fishy fin
And flopped onto the shore.

A million years went quickly by.
The creature's life seemed sweet,
As bit by bit his fins turned into
Wobbly padded feet.
His fishy gills turned into lungs
So he could breathe the air.
"Wow, this is great!" the creature cried.
"I'll wander everywhere!"

Another million years slipped by.
Things didn't go as planned.
The ice age came. The creature cried,
"I hate it here on land!
Though I've become a mammal,
This is not the life for me.
I've decided wet is better!"
Then he flopped back in the sea.

Two more million years zipped by.
His friend cried, "Look at you!
Your feet have turned to flippers now,
Your lungs are bigger, too!
You're a water-dwelling mammal
With a powerful wide tail!"
"Hey, cool," the creature answered,
"I'm the world's first living whale!"

What You Should Answer If Some Scientist Comes Up to You and Says, "What Do All Proboscideans Have in Common?"

Noses
Like hoses.

A Poem About One Way Scientists Tell How Smart Our Ancestors Were: They Measure the Brain Size by Filling the Skull with Uncooked Rice and Then Pouring the Rice into Measuring Cups (Yucch!)

The skull of a human three million years old
Would hold less than two cups of rice.
The skull of a ten-year-old living today
Might hold over six cups, quite nice.
One and a half cups might measure the brain
Of a chimpanzee, frisky and nimble.
And the rice that would measure my sister's brain
Could probably fit in a thimble.

Odd Pair

Tyrannosaurus, king of beasts,
Once ruled the ancient earth,
Huge and nasty, fierce and mean,
With strength of highest worth.

Now in the world at that same time,
On nature's grassy rug,
There crawled the lowly cockroach,
Who is not my favorite bug.

Yes, little roaches scurried down
The path that *T. rex* trod.
The two might pass each other by
Without a word or nod.

Oh mighty *T. rex*, tiny roach!
There's not much more to say,
Except tyrannosaurs are gone…
And roaches live today.

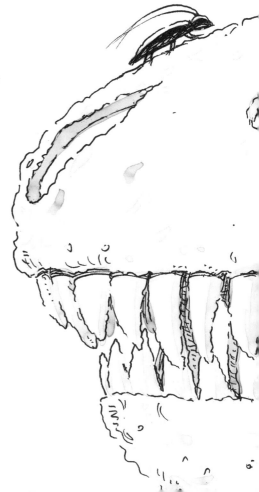

These facts may come in handy
On some prehistoric quiz,
For this story has a lesson...
I'm just not sure what it is.

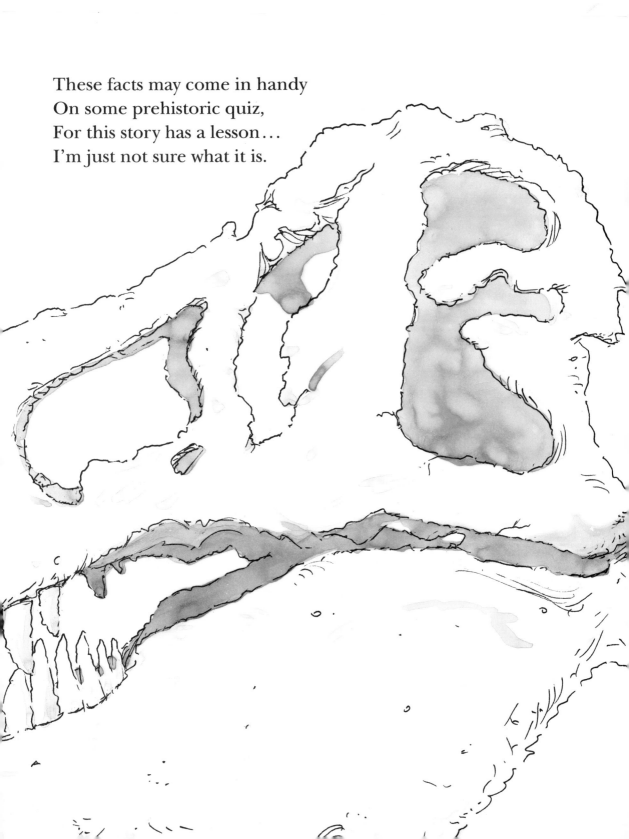

A Long Time (or Sometimes You're Not as Important as You Think)

The earth probably came into being
About four billion years ago.
That's 4
With
Zero-zero-zero-zero-zero-zero-zero-zero-zero
After it.

The first modern human being, *Homo sapiens,*
Appeared on earth
About a hundred thousand years ago.
That's 1
With only
Zero-zero-zero-zero-zero
After it.

Okay, now.

Let's pretend that the earth came into being yesterday
At exactly midnight.
Let's say twenty-four hours have passed since then
And it is now midnight again.
Do you know what time
The first *Homo sapiens* would have arrived?

He would have appeared
At 11:59 p.m. and 57.5 seconds.
Which would mean that so far,
Man has been on earth
For two and a half seconds.

That's about how long it takes my brother to get me mad.

A Poem to Help You Figure Out What Bone the Patella Is

A hairy young primate named Stella
Once yelled, "Ow! I hurt my patella!"
So her mom chimpanzee
Simply bandaged her knee
And made well a patella of Stella.

What the Paleontologist Said When She Uncovered the Biggest Dinosaur Bone She Had Ever Seen

What a colossal
Fossil!

The Evolution of the
Woolly Mammoth

In a snowstorm, a mammoth *un*-woolly
Worried, "Now I'll catch cold proba-bully!"
But in time this big worrier
Became a bit furrier
And eventually grew woolly fully.

Stand Up Straight!

"Stand up straight!" my mother says.
She says it every day.
She doesn't know how hard it is
To try to get that way.
She hasn't read her history
(I'm sure that you've read yours)
About how we once roamed the earth
Crawling on all fours.
It took our ancient relatives
A million years or two
Till they at last succeeded
At what Mom wants me to do.
I've only started recently,
So how can Mom expect
A kid who hasn't practiced
To stand perfectly erect?
But still I'll try my hardest
And I'm sure that I'll succeed.
I'll improve my slumping posture
And I'll do it with great speed.
I'm quicker than those ancient guys—
So Mom, forget your fears!
I'm sure I'll learn to stand up straight…
In less than fifty years!

Mammals:
The Smallest
and The Smartest

The shrew,
and you.

206

A grown-up human being has
  approximately
Two hundred and six different bones
In his or her body.
Can you imagine, then, how many
  different bones
A huge *Tyrannosaurus rex* would have?

Well, a *Tyrannosaurus rex*
Has approximately
Two
Hundred
And six
Different bones
In his or her body—
Same as us.

Hmmmmm...

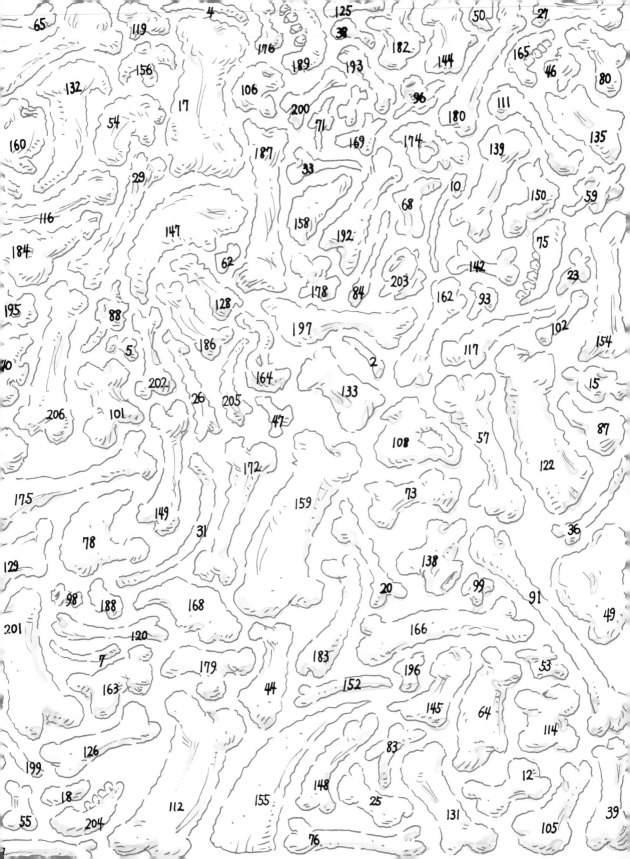

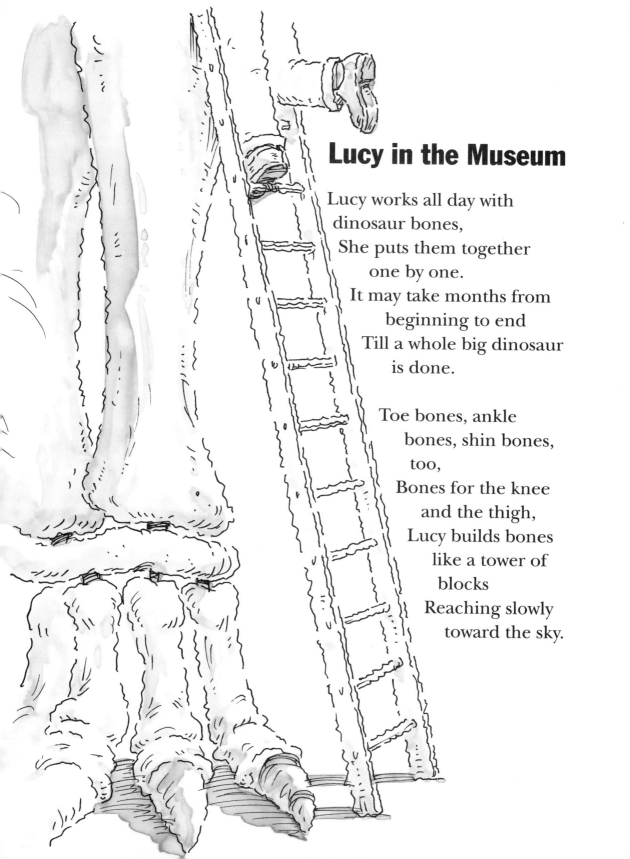

Lucy in the Museum

Lucy works all day with
dinosaur bones,
She puts them together
one by one.
It may take months from
beginning to end
Till a whole big dinosaur
is done.

Toe bones, ankle
bones, shin bones,
too,
Bones for the knee
and the thigh,
Lucy builds bones
like a tower of
blocks
Reaching slowly
toward the sky.

Bones for the hips and bones for the back,
Bones for the ribs and chest,
Onward and upward Lucy goes
On her dinosaur-building quest.

Lucy gets nervous when she nears the top,
She stands on a ladder so tall.
Shoulder bones, neck bones, head bones... Ooops!
Be careful you don't fall.

At last, the final bone is in place,
Lucy lets out a cry.
Then she takes one last deep breath
And climbs back down with a sigh.

Lucy looks up at all those bones,
She's the proudest person in town...
(I wonder if her brother ever comes by
And knocks the whole thing down.)

Something to Think About If Someone Asks You If You Would Like to Move into a Beautiful New House Right Next Door to a Saber-Toothed Tiger Family

Do you really want a neighbor
With teeth like a saber?

Eggs

There are fifty-eight kids in our grade at school.
If each of us wanted scrambled eggs for breakfast,
Here is what we would need:

A two-gallon container to put all the eggy stuff in,
An extra-big fork or eggbeater to stir it all up,
A stove,
A very big frying pan,

And…

One
Large
Dinosaur egg,
Approximately the size of a basketball.

Then all fifty-eight of us could have
A nice scrambled egg breakfast,
And there'd still be enough left over
For our teachers.

I'm Glad That Dinos Are Extinct

I'm glad that dinos are extinct,
I'll gladly tell you why.
If dinos still existed,
Where would we be, you and I?
In fact we wouldn't be here
Nor would any largish mammal,
Not a donkey or gorilla
Not an elephant or camel.
'Cause eighty million years ago,
All mammals had to hide
From the dinos who would eat them
If they ever went outside.
The mammals all were tiny then,
Afraid that they'd get hurt,
Afraid they might end up
As some tyrannosaur's dessert.
Survival for a mammal
Was a problem hard to solve—
As long as dinos ruled the earth
No mammals could evolve.
But after many million years
The great day finally came,
At last the dinos were extinct,
The world was not the same.

The tiny mammals whooped with joy
And had a celebration,
'Cause great new things would now evolve
For each new generation.
First came the early primates,
There were lemurs, monkeys, apes,
The first to grasp things with their hands,
Their brains had larger shapes.
A few more million years went by
Till history could see
The beginnings of amazing creatures
Much like you and me.
Then finally *Homo sapiens*
Could use his or her head
To think and talk and laugh
And make up stories to be read.
So...I'm glad that dinos are extinct,
They're not a group I miss.
'Cause if there still were dinos,
You would not be reading this.

Where to Find Millions of Bones

Go to the museum
And see 'em.

POEMS

POEMS

PRONUNCIATION GUIDE

POEMS

INDEX

ACKNOWLEDGMENTS

POEMS

Answers to Dinosaur Math Quiz on Page 40

1) *Monoclonius* = 1 horn
   Triceratops = 3 horns
   Pentaceratops = 5 horns

2) This is a trick question. There were no trains back then, silly!

3) There are some people who like math quizzes better than poems,
   so why shouldn't they enjoy themselves, too?

Apology for Pages 70–71

If you almost went crazy because you only counted 205 bones
on pages 70 and 71, we're sorry. We made a mistake and left out
bone number 43. Here it is.

Pronunciation Guide

INDEX

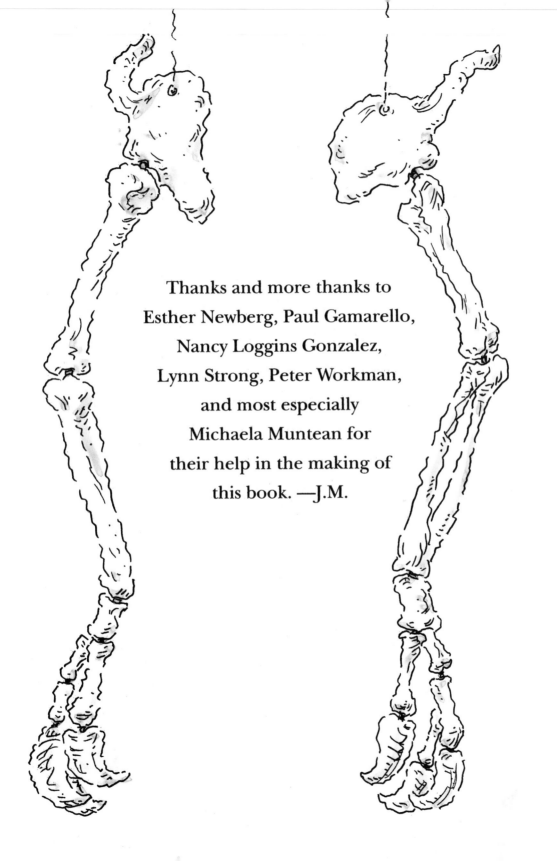

Thanks and more thanks to
Esther Newberg, Paul Gamarello,
Nancy Loggins Gonzalez,
Lynn Strong, Peter Workman,
and most especially
Michaela Muntean for
their help in the making of
this book. —J.M.

The American Museum of Natural History in New York City is home to millions of bones, with one of the largest and most important dinosaur collections in the world. Since the 1890s, Museum scientists have traveled the globe gathering fossils of hundreds of different dinosaurs. Many of these are displayed on the fourth floor of the Museum, where you can visit a huge, open-mouthed *Tyrannosaurus rex*, touch a real dinosaur tooth, and view the mummified skin of *Edmontosaurus*. In the lobby you can stand next to a five-story-tall mount of *Barosaurus* and *Allosaurus*. The Museum has fossils of many of the dinosaurs, pterosaurs, and ancient mammals included in this book. So next time you're in New York, stop by and see the bones of *Stegosaurus, Triceratops, Ankylosaurus, Anatotitan*, a woolly mammoth, and that oh-so-hard-to-pronounce *Quetzalcoatlus*.

Jeff Moss is one of the original creators of *Sesame Street*. He has won fourteen Emmys, written the songs for four Grammy-winning records, was nominated for an Academy Award for the songs in *The Muppets Take Manhattan*, and is the author of the the best-selling poetry collections *The Butterfly Jar* and *The Other Side of the Door*, as well as *Bob and Jack* and *Hieronymus White*, stories in verse. He lives with his wife and son in New York City, very near the American Museum of Natural History.

Tom Leigh has illustrated many *Sesame Street* and Muppet® books, and is also a longtime illustrator of children's educational books. He lives on Little Deer Isle off the coast of Maine with his wife, Susanna, four dogs, and two cats.